HOW NOT TO CARE
WHAT PEOPLE THINK

How Not to Care What People Think

The 4 Steps to Staying True to Yourself

Dr. Tracy®, Ph.D.

Proanoia Publishing

Published by Proanoia Publishing

ISBN 978-1-9798-0029-7

Typesetting services by BOOKOW.COM

CONTENTS

Chapter 1

The Confusion Of Caring

THIS book is called "**How *Not* to Care What People Think.**" But before you begin this unique journey, I need to make one important disclaimer.

Regardless of how it sounds, this book about *not* caring what people think, is *not* a book about *not* caring. Meaning, "**How *Not* to Care What People Think**" is *not* an instruction manual on how to become a lovable Narcissist, or a socialized Sociopath. It's not a "read-the-middle-finger" mémoire that will teach you how to wave your freak flag of selfishness and abandon your life, family, job or responsibilities. Nor is this a book where you will learn the *art* of how to become a less-caring human.

No. "**How *Not* to Care What People Think**", is instead a loving and empowering book written for the over-caring and the tender hearted. Meaning, I wrote this book specifically for those who *worry* more about others, before they worry about themselves. Or, it's for those who've abandoned their inner-calling and dreams because they *fear* losing someone they "love." Or, it's for those who shape-shift or dim-down because their brightness causes others to harshly judge. Or more simply stated, this book about *not* caring what people think, was written for those who *care* too much; *and more important, whose lives are suffering on account of this unbalanced concern.*

I was prompted to write this book about *NOT* caring what people think, because I'm personally guilty of *all* the above charges. In fact, when I reflect on my years of meandering emotional misery, it's easy to see that the catalyst of my pain stemmed, when in the name of God, right, wrong or how it *should* be, *I* abandoned my tribal beats and stripes *for* the sake of others; which for the record, always left me restless and rudderless.

A few years ago though, I came across a book called "The Top Five Regrets of the Dying" by Bronnie Ware. (Hay House Publishers Inc. 2012). The book was a reflective hospice mémoire about the five regrets of the dying, and the *abandoned* choices they never made.

Without a doubt, the five regrets in the book made me think twice about the choices we make, or unfortunately, do *not*. But there was one regret in particular, that jarred me to the core. It was the *primary* regret the dying all collectively mourned, which was the remorse of *not* having the courage to live their lives *true* to themselves, but instead abandoned their life for the *expectations* of others.

I'd like to say I was so deeply moved by the confessions of the dying because I had just turned 50, and certainly after that number, mortality shines brighter in our viewfinder. But the truth-of-the-matter was that I was so stirred by what I read, because their words confirmed something I had *always* known, (yet I hadn't completely honored) which was, *it is downright wrong to abandon our self and our life's journey, for **anyone**.*

About This Book

There are many books on the market that want to give you the five steps to "whatever", and then provide you the long-winding road map on *how* to get there. But **"How Not to Care What People Think"** is not one of those writings.

Instead, **"How Not to Care What People Think"** is a simple, yet easy-to-read mini-book, that has a one-fold intention. That intention is, to share that our birth-right *responsibility* is to step into the highest, most pure definition of Self, so that we can experience authentic joy, authentic love, and our perfect expression of Self, *all while* fulfilling our life's ultimate purpose and contribution. In other words, it is to share *why,* on a *soul* level, our primary life's goal is to evolve into our *Individuality;* and how by *releasing* our concern with what others think, is our path and roadmap to get there.

Why We Care So Much

The question as to *why* we care so much about what others think, is a question we *overly*-caring, ask *way* too often. Here however, is the simple answer to that daunting quandary. The reason we care *so* much about what other people think is (drum roll please): *Because we do.*

The fact-of-the-matter is that as "normal" human beings, we are hard-wired to *care,* and we *cannot* help but be connected, or form emotional bonds, to and with other people, *especially when these people represent certain things to us.* Meaning, especially when they represent things such as our visibility, our sexuality, our salvation, the chance for happiness, our fun, freedom, hope, love, approval, stability, safety, connection, family, identity, femininity, prosperity, or a whole other slew of things that keep us tied.

The bottom line is that as long as we have a heart, *none of us* are exempt from being tethered to someone's opinion, validation, acceptance, appreciation or approval of us.

The question then becomes, how do we *untether* our self from the opinions, judgements and expectations of others and set our self internally free?

Chapter 2

I AM WHO I AM, AND THAT IS GOOD

(Reason #1 to Not Care What People Think)

IN 2002, in need of creating a better self-existence, I unintentionally became a student of thought. It was an exploration that blew open my soul, and changed my life forever.

Of the *many* teachings I learned as a student of thought, the one that affected me the most, was my introduction into the Laws of Creation.

If you're not familiar with The Laws of Creation, they are the universal principles connected with physics, that empower us to *create* the life we desire. In other words, they are a set of laws that due to their scientific foundation, grant us a tremendous amount of *control* over the outcome of our destiny. As a person who spent the majority of my life feeling like a ping-pong ball on the table of life, this insight was *epic*.

Within the Laws of Creation there are four primary laws that make up its infrastructure. They are:

1. The Law of Deliberate Intent

2. The Vacuum Law

3. The Law of Attraction

4. The Law of Allowance

The Law of Allowance

The Law of Allowance is a Universal principle that states, *"I am who I am and that is good; and you are who you are, and I must accept that."*

Like all governing Universal Laws, the Law of Allowance serves a primary life purpose, which is to navigate us *from within*, to our *Soul's* Purpose. In layman's term, its job is to navigate us to our *Individuality*.

Experts say that the Law of Allowance is the most difficult Universal Law to learn. However, they also say that if you manage to master the disciplines of this Law, it has the power to change both the trajectory as well as the *quality* of your life. Speaking from first-hand experience, I fully agree.

The Law of Allowance teaches us, that each person who enters this physical existence comes (here) with the goal of learning specific lessons, for the primary purpose of *expanding* our Soul.

The Law imparts two very important lessons about Individuality. First, it teaches us that we are all on an individual journey, and as such, no *two* journeys are ever alike. That is why the law reads, "I am who I am, and that is good." It is an unapologetic expression of our *Individuality*.

At the same time, the Law also teaches us that, as the primary purpose of our individual journey is to learn *our* specific soul lessons, *none of us* are to control, manipulate, detour, or stop another person from fulfilling their Souls' Purpose. That is why the Law continues by saying, "You are who you are, *and I must accept that.*" It too, is an unapologetic acceptance of *others Individuality.*

Most people can easily embrace the first part of the Law of Allowance, in that they love, love, love the idea of having *their* Individuality.

Unfortunately however, that same adoration doesn't always transfer to the second part of the teaching; where rather than us *allowing* each person to grow and expand into their pre-designed authentic purpose, most of us are guilty of vice- gripping our personal agendas, beliefs and expectations onto others, by trying to navigate, manipulate and dictate their outcomes, to fit our personal needs. Or worse, *we allow others to get their emotional hands on us, and dictate ours.*

Is it Real?

If you've never been exposed to the Law of Allowance, it's tempting to discount its authenticity; especially if your religious trainings (or lack there-of) have not allowed you to embrace the concept of a soul's journey, the possibility of multiple-life experiences, or the fact that Divine purpose really exists.

But if you step back from your religious, cultural or foundational programming and you allow yourself to *listen* to your body's spiritual and physical communication system, the Law of Allowance's *"pushes-and-pulls"* are nearly impossible to ignore.

For example, the Law has *pushed* on our Soul when the culture we were born into, or the religion we were raised with, or the body we were given, just never felt aligned. Or, we have felt the Law's *pull* when our feet touched foreign land and we could *breathe* for the first time. Or when we discovered a passion that cracked open our First Voice. Or when we first prayed to a Source that felt authentically real. Or when our lips tasted love, versus just a kiss, for the very first time.

If and when we're *not* aware of the Law's existence, our initial response to its inner promptings, is to push *away* or ignore its messages; which we typically *attempt* to do by denying our emotions. Or by smothering ourselves in guilt. Or by harshly and *jealously* judging those who have bravely gone before us. Or we do it by cutting off our dreams, disconnecting from that which makes us feel, or worse, we do it by slipping into a life-long battle with depression because we *know* deep inside we've abandoned our self.

But here is a Memo from Normal Land® regarding the purpose of our Soul: *Our Soul has been hard-wired to seek us from the time we were born; and its commitment to Self will **never die.***

Meaning, until the day you take your final breath, your Soul will pursue you like a mother with a lost child, where she will *not* stop, will not sleep, nor will she abandon her search and connection with you, until you give her birth, breath and life.

Clearly stated, your Soul will *not* stop tapping at your heart *until* you evolve into the highest, most pure definition of Self. She will not stop until you step into who you have *Divinely* been called here to become. And she will not stop pursuing you until you *contribute* what you have Divinely been designed to donate.

The purpose of our Soul is to give *life* to our Individuality. That's why the Memo from Normal Land® says, *"It is both our right and responsibility to fulfill our individual Soul's purpose"*; a purpose that *in spite* of who approves, *in spite* of who disapproves, and most important, *in spite* of what *anyone* thinks, is our right and *responsibility* to pursue.

Memo from Normal Land®
It is both our right and responsibility to fulfill our individual Soul's purpose."

Chapter 3

IT'S NOT PERSONAL

(Reason #2 to Not Care What People Think)

THERE's no question that caring is *not* for the faint-hearted; especially for we *Feelers or Empaths* who take life *in* the heart. We know first-hand how much it *hurts* when people we care about, *don't* care about us.

I was reminded of this lesson last summer during one of my workshops, when a young girl named Ashley was dialoguing about some bullying she endured from a group of girls who were once her friends. She was a few sentences into her share when the years of internalized pain and abuse welled to the surface, and with it came tears of hurt, loss, shame and confusion.

I asked Ashley to tell me more about these former friends of hers, where in-turn she described a group of young women who engaged in gossip, gas lighting, character assassination, and more.

When she was finished, I looked at Ashley with her tear-stained eyes and raw rejection wounds and bluntly said, "Ashley, I'm so *glad* they have an issue with you."

My words stunned the room into silence.

Tribal Colors

I am part Native-American. A card-carrying Cherokee Indian to be exact.

As a Cherokee Indian, my tribe is just one of the hundreds scattered across the Americas. Though each Nation is uniquely identified by it's different colors, traditions and personalities, I happen to be most proud of my Cherokee roots. Why? Because as a Sovereign Nation, we are known as the tribe of *peace*.

I mention my tribal affiliation because we as humans are *all* tribal beings. As such, it's within our nature to find our *tribal connection*. Meaning, be it identifying with our culture, or our religion, or even the color of our hair, we *all* by nature seek tribal affiliations to feel more visible, united and connected.

If you doubt that concept, just look around: We join sport teams and wear the same colors as a sign of unity. We become members of sororities and claim the same name as a sisterhood. We affiliate with churches and political parties to align our beliefs with those of the same convictions. And (including the case of the nasty girls), some even join clicks with similar souls, who reflect our *personal* values and worth.

That however is exactly *why* we don't need to take things personal, or allow another person's *judgment* to get under our skin. In case you didn't get the Memo from Normal Land® regarding people's behavior: *"How a person treats us, is never really about us."* Believe it or not, their behavior is simply a *projection* of their personal beliefs, character, aches, pains, fears, values or worth, that they *throw* at us. In other words, how they behave towards us, is a reflection of *their* emotional inventory, not ours.

Memo from Normal Land®
How a person treats us is never really about us.

And this concept holds true from the bully on the play-ground, to the partner who rejects us, to even the horrific Hitler's of the world. *The opinions of others have nothing to do with us.* Instead, their external actions are reflections of *their* internal (sometimes tormented) selves.

But what if their opinion of us causes us pain? The answer is that we can only be hurt by another person's words and actions if we *align*, or agree with what they say is *true*.

For example, if somebody says we are "a big zero" (or a big turd, idiot or dummy) and deep inside *we believe* we are, then that *alignment* puts us in their camp of truth, and therefore, launches our personal pain. Or, if someone treats us as though they are better than us, and we *align* with it by internally believing we are *less-than*, their actions will then have the power to cut us to the core.

However, if we are *clear* on our personal truths, meaning that we understand who we *are,* and who we *are not,* (known as our *Individuality*) then the comments and behaviors of others are defused to nothing more than *opinions*. Opinions that I prefer to call, "cheesy-moon" moments.

I call them cheesy-moon moments because if a person wants to believe that the moon is made of cheese, according to the Law of Allowance, I must *accept* that opinion as theirs. However, if *my* truth tells me that the moon is *not* made of cheese (which is my right) no matter how much they want to *think* I am "stupid" because I don't agree with them, I am left unshaken by their judgement or name-calling; *because* I know my truth, which is, the moon is *not* made of cheese. Just as I *also* know my hair color doesn't equate to my intelligence. My race or gender doesn't make me less-than, my paycheck doesn't set my value, and my bra size doesn't make me a better or less-than woman.

I am so grounded in this concept of *not* taking things personal because a few years ago I learned an *excellent* Memo from Normal Land® about pushy people with strong opinions. It says: *"Just because they say it, doesn't make it true."*

Memo from Normal Land®
Just because they say it, doesn't make it true.

It's a life-skill called "Individuality Awareness" where at *all* times we possess the power to be grounded in our Soul's purpose, and choose to ignore another person's opinions. Or, we can abandon our Individuality, and align with their messages and be destroyed.

The choice of *how* we react rests 100% within us, and it is based in our personal awareness of our *Individuality*. Or in other words, it is based in who we believe we are, and who we know we are *not*.

But what happens if we are good with our self, yet a person's behavior still bothers us? Well, my advice is to consider the same feedback I gave Ashley, which is this:

If on the playground of life, the cruel girls (or guys) don't find us "acceptable", good enough, or someone worthy of their world, do we really *need* to care what these people think of us? Meaning, at the end of the day, do we *really* want the stamp of *approval* from a person whose values, opinions, and treatment don't feel right, pure or good to us? Do we really need to be concerned about the opinion of someone who needs *us* to be a *lesser* version of Self, to make *them* feel bigger? Or, when it comes to the people who need to harm, or insult, or *breakdown* another human, so their world feels safe, is this someone we *really* want to "align" our standards, integrity, or value with?

I say, "No."

I say, "Let's not take their *shitiness* personal."

I say, rather than get our feelings hurt, or step into self-loathing, or abandon our Authentic Self, let's instead move towards a kinder thought that says, maybe their jack-ass behavior is part of *their* master lesson, that *they* came here to learn. Or even better yet, maybe learning to *not* let their opinion *affect* me, is part of mine.

I say, Memo from Normal Land®: "*When it comes to not caring what people think, let's remember that we are not required to align with anything, or anyone that doesn't feel right, good, or pure to us.* Not because we are better or worse than anyone; but because according to the Law of Allowance we are all *individually* made. And *in spite* of what others think, that is a very *good* thing.

Chapter 4

IT'S ALL ABOUT AUTHENTIC LOVE

(Reason #3 to Not Care What People Think)

FOR several years I was in an abusive marriage. It was an overly controlling relationship where my *then* husband was telling me how to think, what to think, and why I should think it.

I knew during those overly-controlling years that his abusive behavior wasn't correct. But somewhere between my religious indoctrination, combined with my drowning levels of abandonment pain, I felt forced to stay in a relationship where I was accepting the unacceptable, and tolerating the intolerable.

During those less-than loving years, I did something many abandoned-infused souls do: I shaped-shifted and dimmed down to make others feel comfortable.

For example, if my smile made yours look dim, I would turn down my 'dents' so you could shine brighter. Or, if my passion for dreams highlighted the abandonment of yours, I would hide my desires to make you feel okay.

Unfortunately, I never thought twice about shape-shifting for others during that powerless time. That's because as an abandoned-based soul, I was desperate for the love and acceptance of others. In fact somewhere along my journey, I came to believe that "the love of others" was the end-all, and *be-all* cure to my debilitating internal pain. Or as I preferred to call it, "It was the *cure* to that daunting *hole in my soul*, that I had lugged around inside me since the beginning of time."

Out of the Darkness

I am a big dreamer. But not just a day-time, "create your life by design" dreamer. I am also a 3-D, surround-sound, *night time* dreamer as well.

When I close my eyes and slip into my sleep state, my soul enters a land of adventure some could only wish to experience. I fly. I power swim and breathe under water. I see people from my past. I solve daytime problems. And I even get spiritual "downloads" (as I call them) that give me insight and wisdom I could never find while consciously awake.

One evening during my sleep-ventures I got a Dream Download, where I was in a dark tunnel, slowly yet pensively walking towards a bright light.

Before I continue, I need to share that during that season I had been passionately working on becoming *congruent*. Meaning, my emotional goal was to become "One Tracy / Multiple Audiences." In other words, I was committed to becoming the same person on the *inside*, that I presented to the outside world.

I had gone through many layers of emotional shedding up to that point, so as my dream unfolded, I immediately understood it's symbologies: The darkness of the tunnel represented the dimmed-down version of me. The passage was my transition to change. And the light waiting for me at the tunnel opening, was me stepping into my Authentic Self.

When my dream began, I remember my body being consumed with fear because *(as dreams are)* the hole-in-my soul had been speaking to me. "She" was afraid because apparently, we had been living in the darkness for years. But again *(as dreams are)* something had changed, and there was an pressing urgency for me to exit the tunnel.

With every step I took towards the guiding light, my emotions toggled back and forth, where in one step I was filled with excitement and breath as I imagined entering into the light as my Authentic Self. Then in the next step, I would be *consumed* with crippling fear, because *who* if anyone, would be waiting and *accepting* of the Authentic Me?

I don't recall exactly how my dream ended that night, but I do remember the life-shifting lesson it taught me that next day. It was a lesson based on Authentic Love, and how the only way we can *experience* its amazing beauty, is to have the courage to show-up as our Authentic Self; because only *when* we show-up as our Authentic Self, will we discover who is *really* there for us. Which to an abandoned soul (who desperately worries about what people think) is one of the *most* valuable lessons we can ever learn.

That night in the tunnel I learned the Memo from Normal Land® about Authentic Love that says, "*Those who authentically love us, will be there.*" Non-judgmentally waiting at the tunnel door, excited and *all*-accepting of the "flawed-to- fantastic" person called You. And *clearly* letting us know by their physical presence alone, that we will *never* have to wonder who is really *there*. Meaning, our mind won't have to worry about what they might *think, or* our emotions won't have to toggle in fear or concern, because if they are waiting for us at the tunnel door, it means they really do authentically care, because of the physical evidence that they are authentically *there*.

Memo from Normal Land®
*Those who authentically love us, are **there**.*

Chapter 5

BECAUSE I'M CHOCOLATE

(Reason #4 to Not Care What People Think)

S EVERAL years ago, I learned something unique about myself. I discovered that I am Chocolate. Meaning, if my emotional DNA had a flavor, it would be chocolate.

As an *ever-evolving* Chocolate, I'm constantly working on expanding myself into something new. For example, one year I might be a chocolate soufflé. The next year, maybe a chocolate milk shake. And the next year, I might evolve into a chocolate brownie. But there is one thing for sure about the Authentic Me: As my emotional DNA *is* chocolate, I will *always* be a version of chocolate.

I didn't know this about myself for a very long time. And during those unconscious years I let the *Orange-ies* in life, make me feel bad about my chocolateness.

For example, the Orange-ies would look at my mysterious cocoa ways and scream, "What is *wrong* with you?! Don't you know being an Orange-ie is the *better* way!! " Then in the effort to become "*better" or more accepted*, I dimmed-down, shaped- shifted, changed my color, produced Vitamin C; only to wake-up one day with cancer.

I want to make one thing perfectly clear. There is *nothing* wrong with being an Orange-ie. In fact, I love Orange-ies, and I know they make the world go around. But that being said, for us to shape-shift our self into another person's version of right, or to *care too much* what the Orange-ies think; or to be concerned because they don't "get" the *not* normal ways of a Chocolate, is simply *not* how this journey is supposed to work. In case you didn't get the Memo from Normal Land®: W*e all have the right to enjoy this journey called life, even if we come in a package others don't understand.*"

Memo from Normal Land®
*We all have the right to enjoy this journey called life,
even if we come in a package others don't understand.*

The Joyous Journey of Not Caring

If you're familiar with my professional work, you know that my heart's passion is to teach people the Journey to Self-Love. What you might not know is the reason I'm so in "in love" with this work is because I spent *years* of my life, living *out* of love with myself. The unfortunate result of that disconnected time, was a life built on giving to others, more than I gave to myself; a life where I listened to others, more than I listened to myself; and an existence where I did for others, more than I did for myself.

I've questioned over the years *where* my life would be today, had I given myself the same amount of love I granted to others; or in the case of this book, how *differently* would my life had been had I cared *less* about what others think, and more about myself?

Without pause, I *know* the answer: Depression would have been an occasional visitor, rather than a permanent house guest. The dreams

I waited decades to arrive, would have blossomed years earlier. Love would have been a much gentler path because authenticity would have been its base. And stress-related sickness would have had no gateway to manifest itself in my body.

There's no doubt that when Jesus said, *"Love your neighbor as yourself"*, or the Buddha said, *"You, as much as anybody in the entire universe, deserve your love and affection"*, they both were prescribing the keys to emotional wellness.

However, all that said, where do we find the balance? Meaning, as love based individuals who *do* care how our choices affect other's lives, how do we turn-down our "care-too-much-thermometer" and step into the "no-care" zone, all *without* compromising our compassion or concern for others? Or in other words, how do we learn how *not* to care what other's think, and yet remain a loving *individual*? Where does the balance in *caring what others think*, versus *self*-care reside?

I believe the answer is found in what I call the 4 R's of Not Caring What People Think.

The 4 R's of Not Caring What People Think
(Creating the Shift from Them to You)

The 4 R's of Not Caring What People Think is a roadmap of empowerment, where we learn *how* to love and care in *deeper* ways, by shifting our focus *away* from others, and putting the love directly onto our self.

The 4 R's of Not Caring What People Think includes Re-directing, Re-routing, Releasing and Realigning.

1) **Re-directing**: When a plane is on the wrong landing approach, the air traffic controllers will *re-direct* the pilots to their proper landing quadrants. To ensure a safe landing, the pilots need to simply *listen* to the instructions they hear in their headphones, and follow the air traffic controllers advice.

Step one in shifting *away* from caring what others think, *to focusing more on caring for Self*, works much the same way.

It's a step called *Re-directing* and it's a discipline where we *re-direct* our "headphones" *away* from those who tether us with guilt, pressure, and agendas, and shift our focus *towards* the Heavens for guidance.

Re-directing is an important first step in the journey to caring more for Self, because this slight spiritual shift aligns us with something called *Divine Order.*

Divine Order is a Spiritual Law that states, "There is a perfect solution already in place, as long as I align myself with it."

Divine Order is such an amazing course to follow because when we operate in its perfect structure, the answer to what is best for *all*, will present itself. In other words, when we look to Divine Order for our answers, we will find the win/win, the "perfect solution", the safe landing, and the happy ending for *everyone*. Which to a person who cares too much what people think, leaves us with the feel-good.

2) **Re-routing**: Recently I was driving from Long Beach, California to my home town of Newport Beach. Unexpectedly, the freeway I was traveling on had a late-night road closure. In spite of me being geographically handicap, I didn't panic because on command, my GPS automatically *re-routed* me, and found a *new* way home.

The next step in shifting *away* from caring what others think, *to focusing more on caring for Self,* is called *Re-routing.*

Re-routing is a discipline where we consciously *re-route* our life-path, from that of living at a *disconnect* from Self (a.k.a. in the tunnel) onto living the path of Self Authenticity.

Re-routing is similar to pressing a reset button, where you "shake out the carpet" on yourself, and get current with who you are *today.* It's the season where you shed *anything* that no longer best serves you, and where you intentionally re-invent yourself into a modern-day version of Self.

Re-routing your "person" as well as your path is paramount to re-claiming *your* life because Memo from Normal Land®: *When we get a firm grip on our self, we no longer allow people to keep their grip on us.* This then puts an *untangling* effect into motion because when people get their emotional hands off us, it empowers us to do what we've been called here to do. But better, it also frees those who are over-occupied with us, to do what *they* have come here to do as well.

In a sense, *Re-routing* clears out the traffic jams of life, because through this beautiful reset, it puts everyone in their *own* life-lane, which according to Divine Purpose, is how things are supposed to be.

Memo from Normal Land®:
When we get a firm grip on our self,
we no longer allow people to keep their grip on us.

3) **Releasing:** For the past twenty-ne years I have worked in the world of abuse recovery. Needless to say, over that time I've seen

a lot of Love Trauma Wounds. However, no matter how bad or painful a person's experience with love has been, my end goal on the recovery journey remains the same: "Love *is* the Goal."

The third step in shifting *away* from caring what others think, *to focusing more on caring for Self*, is the *loving* act of *Releasing*.

Releasing is the physical step of giving back to the Universe *anyone who doesn't love us in our entirety, in order to make room for someone who does.*

I know for an abandoned soul, *Releasing* feels like shooting our self in the foot, because we will do almost anything for love. But when someone's partial love (known as *segmented* love) leaves us questioning love, or pining for love, or constantly repairing our mind, heart or body over someone's love, this not only takes up too much brain space, but worse, it keeps us at the *mercy* of another person's opinion and or acceptance of us; which this is *not* love, at all.

Releasing is such an important step on the journey to *not* caring what people think, because as my mother has always instilled in me, "If love has become too difficult, you're doing it wrong." *Releasing* those who only partially love us, is our gateway to getting Love *right*.

4) **Realigning**: If you have ever injured your back, you know the *great* relief you experience when the Chiropractor "realigns" you. You can walk upright. You can move freely. In general, you get the power to navigate your life back.

The fourth and final step in shifting *away* from caring what others think, *to focusing more on caring for Self*, is called *Realigning*.

Realigning is the act of *reclaiming* your Emotional Posture. In other words, it's learning to stand *upright* and straight, from within. *Realigning* is taking ownership of your life, as the Boss of You. It's the act of claiming your rightful space, without apology. Or as I said earlier, it's embracing that as a unique Soul and Individual, you are Chocolate.

Memo from Normal Land®:
Chocolate is the new normal.

Realigning is such an important step in *not* caring what people think because when we embrace our Chocolate and *Realign* with our Individuality, our feet finally touch ground on the road Divinely designed for us.

It's a road called our *Soul's Authentic Path,* and its one where without effort, we will find our authentic love (in other words, our chocoholics), we will discover our authentic joy (meaning the things in life that make us as say, "I love this"). And it's a road where we will continue grow into the highest, most pure definition of Self.

The best part about this amazing path however, is that once we are on it, we will *never* have to worry what others think again. Not because we *don't* care what others think. But instead because our landing papers came with the Memo from Normal Land® that says, "As a soul who's been put here for a Divine purpose, *you have the right to be You; and I have the right to be Me; and we all have the right to experience this journey, without any apology.*"

Made in the USA
San Bernardino, CA
11 May 2020